Where Does My Shadow Sleep?

A Parents' Guide to Exploring Science with Children's Books

by Sally Anderson with the Vermont Center for the Book

Also by the Vermont Center for the Book:

Social Studies and Me! Using Children's Books to Learn About Our World

How Many Ways Can You Make Five? A Parents' Guide to Exploring Math with Children's Books

Math and Science Investigations: Helping Young Learners Make Big Discoveries

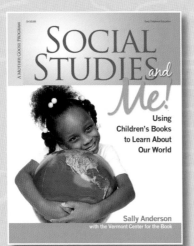

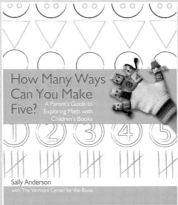

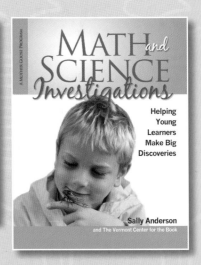

Where Does My Shadow Sleep?

A Parents' Guide to Exploring Science with Children's Books

by Sally Anderson with the Vermont Center for the Book

Illustrations by Mary Rojas
Photography by iStock Photography
Gryphon House, Inc.
Lewisville, NC

Published by Gryphon House, Inc.
PO Box 10, Lewisville, NC 27023
800.638.0928; 877.638.7576 (fax)

Visit us on the web at www.gryphonhouse.com.

Library of Congress Cataloging-in-Publication Data
Anderson, Sally.
 Where does my shadow sleep? : a parent's guide to exploring science with c=
hildren's books / by Sally Anderson with the Vermont Center for the Book.
    pages cm
 Includes bibliographical references and index.
 ISBN 978-0-87659-387-5
 1. Science--Study and teaching (Early childhood)--Activity programs. I. V=
ermont Center for the Book, issuing body. II. Title.
  LB1139.5.S3A54 2012
  372.35--dc23
                                    2012004436

Table of Contents

Introduction

Science Is Everywhere!
Why Use Children's Books to Talk about Science?
Science All the Time

Science Is Everywhere!

Young children are curious; they want to know why things happen, so they can understand their world. They naturally ask the very same questions scientists ask: *Why? How? When? What will happen if...?* Believe it or not, when your child helps you measure ingredients in the kitchen, when you make paper airplanes together, and when she watches an ant and then says, "Come quick and see what this ant is doing!" you are doing science! Young children investigate the world around them just as scientists do.

▸ They make predictions: a seedling will grow into a flower by the end of the summer.

▸ They use materials and tools in creative ways: measure a tower of blocks with a piece of rope.

▸ They observe things carefully: watch ants as they carry crumbs to an anthill.

▸ They solve problems: try to get a blanket to be the roof on a playhouse.

▸ They repeat actions over and over: fill a cup with water, pour it into a hole, fill a cup with water, pour it into a hole, and so on.

Take time to watch, wonder, ask questions, talk about, and explore the world with your child. You don't need to have all the answers! Encourage your child to ask questions, and then explore possible answers with her.

Why Use Children's Books to Talk about Science?

Stories are a powerful and fun way to explore science with your child. Many picture books lend themselves to discussion and exploration of science concepts. For example, you can read a great book such as *Moonbear's Shadow* by Frank Asch. Then you and your child can explore shadows together. How is a shadow made? What does a shadow look like when the sun comes up in the morning? How does a shadow change as the day goes on? Or read *The Man Who Walked between the Towers* by Mordecai Gerstein, and experiment with building towers together. How high can you build? How can you make your tower stronger so it won't fall over?

Where Does My Shadow Sleep? links great children's books—which you are probably already reading with your child—with easy, fun-filled activities to explore the world of science with her. The activities in *Where Does My Shadow Sleep?* were developed for children ages four and older, but most of them also work well with younger children, and most can be done over and over. Give your child a chance to do each one several times, perhaps in different seasons or in different locations or with different materials. Note the changes in her abilities and interests over time. Check out the bibliography at the end of this book, where you will find lots of book suggestions to investigate with your child. *Where Does My Shadow Sleep?* will help you and your child have fun reading about, talking about, and exploring the science in your everyday lives.

Science All the Time

As you and your child talk about and explore scientific processes, skills, and content, you will be acting just like scientists!

Talking Together

▸ Talk about the things you see in your world, such as the weather, animal behaviors, plants, and clouds.

▸ Talk about how characters in books solve their problems.

▸ Wonder aloud and ask questions relating to your activities.

▸ Encourage your child to estimate height, weight, size, time, and speed.

▸ Encourage your child to predict what will happen next, and then see if she is right!

▸ Encourage your child to form a possible explanation (the scientific word is *hypothesis*) for why something is happening.

▸ Allow plenty of time to discuss the investigations you are doing.

▸ Talk about the questions you have about your indoor and outdoor environments.

▸ Look for patterns and sequences in everyday activities: *After we have breakfast, what happens next?*

▸ Ask questions about different objects and experiences: *How is this one different? How is it the same?*

Reading Together

▶ Read biographies of scientists.

▶ Read books about insects, trees, shadows, and other scientific areas of interest.

▶ Make predictions about what will happen next in stories.

▶ Read game instructions or other instructions aloud with your child.

▶ Follow a recipe from a cookbook.

Because our world is filled with opportunities to explore science concepts, science is all around us. Young children naturally learn science concepts through play and interactions with the adults in their lives. Use the ideas in this book as a springboard for enjoying the world of science with your child.

1

Let's Build It!

Let's Build It!

Much of the environment we live in is constructed—not just buildings, but roads, bridges, communication towers, and other structures. These structures are the results of science and mathematics being applied in the disciplines of design and engineering. Structures are designed and built to serve utilitarian functions as well as to please the eye.

When children build, they learn about the importance of balance and strength, the properties of materials, and good design. Here are some examples of how you and your child can explore building and construction:

▶ Explore and compare the properties of a variety of different building materials.

▶ Decide what function a building will have, and design and build a structure to meet that need.

▶ Explore different design elements to make buildings stronger and more stable.

▶ Describe your buildings and what you were thinking of when you built them.

▶ Find opportunities to compare, measure, and count as you build your structures.

Problem Solving

Problem solving is a thinking process that is used in all science learning. Because of their natural curiosity, children approach problems with great enthusiasm. Encourage your child to solve problems in his own way, to think about what is needed to solve the problem, and to use a variety of problem-solving approaches. To help, you might ask:

Why did you decide to do that?

What else do you need?

What if you tried a different material?

How can you change it?

The investigations and conversations in this section will help your child explore methods and develop the perseverance needed to solve problems as he builds a variety of structures and objects.

Books

A classic tale such as *The Three Little Pigs* is an excellent story about building and construction. Design, trial and error, problem solving—all of these science topics are part of the story! Here are a few more recommendations:

Albert's Alphabet by Leslie Tryon

Changes, Changes by Pat Hutchins

A House Is a House for Me by Mary Ann Hoberman

The House in the Meadow by Shutta Crum

Let's Try It Out with Towers and Bridges by Seymour Simon

The Three Little Javelinas by Susan Lowell

The Three Little Pigs by Paul Galdone

Building with Blocks

Talk about the blocks, their shapes, sizes, and positions, as you combine them into a variety of shapes and structures.

Great Books to Read Before Doing This Activity

Block City by Robert Louis Stevenson
Changes, Changes by Pat Hutchins
The Three Little Pigs by Paul Galdone

What's Needed

building blocks
drawing materials

How to Do It

1. Put out all the blocks, and together begin exploring and building.

2. Talk about what your child is building. Here are some ways to start the conversation:

   Tell me about your building.

   Why did you use this block here?

   I notice you used two rectangles. How many different kinds of blocks did you use?

   What do you think would happen if…?

3. Take time to look at and discuss each other's buildings. Ask:

   Which building is tallest? shortest?

   How can we measure our buildings?

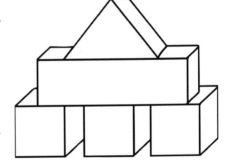

4. Make drawings of your buildings to display for the rest of your family to see.

Copy My Construction

Copy each other's designs by noticing details, placing and naming blocks, and following directions.

Great Books to Read Before Doing This Activity

Changes, Changes by Pat Hutchins
Shapes in Buildings by Rebecca Rissman
The Wing on a Flea by Ed Emberley

What's Needed

variety of blocks

How to Do It

1. Build a simple structure of three blocks, and describe it as you add pieces.
2. When you are finished, ask your child to make the same shaped structure. (The colors might not be the same, depending on the blocks you have available.)
3. Take turns building and copying each other's structures, using more blocks for more complex structures.

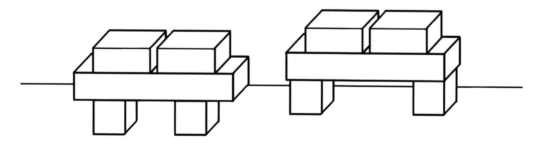

Listen and Build

When your child is able to copy your structures, try this more challenging activity.

Great Books to Read Before Doing This Activity
Changes, Changes by Pat Hutchins
Shapes in Buildings by Rebecca Rissman
The Wing on a Flea by Ed Emberley

What's Needed
book or file folder
variety of blocks

How to Do It
1. Stand a book or a folder in front of where you are building to hide your structure from view.
2. Build a simple structure, and describe it as you build:
   - *First, I put down a rectangle block with a long side touching the table.*
   - *Next, I place a cylinder on end in the middle of the rectangle.*
   - *Third, I put a small triangle prism on top of the cylinder.*
3. As you build and describe your building process, challenge your child to build this same structure without seeing it, using only the verbal directions. This can be much more difficult than using our eyes to see and copy a structure. Building a structure using only verbal cues requires an understanding of specific vocabulary relating to shape (*square, triangle,* and so on) and position (*over, under, next to,* and so on).

Towering Towers

Build towers as you combine and balance shapes, changing the design as you go, to solve any problems you encounter.

Great Books to Read Before Doing This Activity

Let's Try It Out with Towers and Bridges by Seymour Simon
The Man Who Walked between the Towers by Mordecai Gerstein
Sky Boys by Deborah Hopkinson

What's Needed

building blocks
drawing materials

How to Do It

1. Talk as you build the towers, asking questions such as the following:

    ▸ *What shapes can we use to make a strong base?*

    ▸ *How did you keep the tower from falling down?*

    ▸ *What do you think will happen if…?*

    ▸ *What do you think is the most important block in a tower? Why?*

    ▸ *How can we find out if the tower is strong?*

2. Measure your towers using standard and nonstandard units, and make a chart.

    ▸ *How many paper clips tall is your tower?*

    ▸ *How many plastic spoons tall?*

    ▸ *How many inches tall?*

3. Make drawings of your towers and display them with your measurements.

How tall are our towers?			
	#of ✏	#of ▢	#of 📏
Mom's tower	12	5	18
Julia's tower	18	7	27

Building with Purpose

Build a structure for a specific purpose, such as a garage for a toy truck, a house for a giraffe, or a house for an elephant.

Great Books to Read Before Doing This Activity
A House Is a House for Me by Mary Anne Hoberman
The House That Max Built by Maxwell Newhouse
How a House Is Built by Gail Gibbons

What's Needed
blocks
nonstandard measuring tools, such as paper clips, string, or straws

How to Do It
1. Talk about why you are building a specific structure.
2. Talk with your child about his design. Ask questions such as the following:
   ▸ *How big do you think the building should be?*
   ▸ *What do you think will happen if...?*
   ▸ *How will the (truck, giraffe, elephant) get in and out?*
3. Use a nonstandard measuring tool to measure the structure and the creature or vehicle it is for. Ask your child to compare the measurements. Will the (truck, giraffe, elephant) fit inside the structure?

Building Math and Science Skills with Blocks

Measuring, estimating, and comparing are some of the math and science skills children practice when they explore and build with blocks.

▶ *How many blocks tall can I make this?*

▶ *Which tower is the tallest? Which is the shortest?*

▶ *Is the house for the dog taller or shorter than the house for the giraffe?*

▶ *Will I need more or fewer straws for this bridge?*

▶ *How long is your bridge?*

▶ *Which bridge will hold the most pennies?*

▶ *Let's measure our house with paper clips. How many paper clips tall is your house? Is it taller than mine?*

Any book, discussion, or activity that helps your child do the following will meet the educational standards addressing the concept of measurement:

▶ Recognize and understand the concepts of length and time.

▶ Compare and order objects according to length and time.

▶ Understand how to measure using nonstandard units (paper clips, blocks, chopsticks, a piece of string) and standard units (inches, feet, seconds, minutes).

▶ Select an appropriate unit and tool for the feature being measured.

▶ Measure with multiple copies of units of the same size, such as paper clips placed end to end.

▶ Use repetition of a single unit to measure something larger than the unit.

▶ Make comparisons and estimate by using common units of measurement: This toy is four blocks tall, but that doll is six blocks tall.

Building Bridges

Experiment with building bridges of different materials, and make a record of how many objects each bridge can hold.

Great Books to Read Before Doing This Activity

Bridges Are to Cross by Philemon Sturges
Let's Try It Out with Towers and Bridges by Seymour Simon
Twenty-One Elephants and Still Standing by April Jones Prince

What's Needed

8½" x 11" sheets of paper
drawings or photos of bridges
objects of equal weight (pennies or blocks) to test the strength of the bridges
solid blocks or paper cups

How to Do It

1. Look at and talk about some drawings or photos of real bridges. Ask your child some questions, such as the following:

   ▸ *Why do we use bridges?*

   ▸ *Where do we use bridges?*

   ▸ *What shapes do you see in bridge construction?*

   ▸ *A bridge can be as simple as a log across a stream or as complex as the interconnected towers and cables of the Golden Gate Bridge.*

2. Use paper cups or columns of blocks to create the span of your bridge. Use a flat sheet of paper for your first bridge.

3. Test its strength. Ask your child how many objects she thinks the bridge can hold, and help her test her estimate.

4. Experiment building different paper bridges:

   ▸ *Arch the paper,*

   ▸ *Pleat (make multiple folds in) the paper, or*

   ▸ *Use more than one sheet of paper.*

5. Brainstorm ways you could make a bridge stronger. What materials, other than paper, might you use? Try out your ideas.

6. Test the strength of each bridge. How many objects can each bridge hold? Which bridge holds the most weight?

Building with Recycled Materials

Build using a variety of materials, and explore the materials' properties before you begin building a specific object or structure.

Great Books to Read Before Doing This Activity

Albert's Alphabet by Leslie Tryon
Shape Capers by Cathryn Falwell
The Three Little Javelinas by Susan Lowell

What's Needed

glue
paper
recycled or found materials such as shoeboxes, paper towel tubes, paper
   cups, straws, egg cartons, cereal boxes, and clean yogurt containers and lids
scissors
tape

How to Do It

1. Look at and talk about your materials. Compare and discuss the attributes (characteristics) of each material, such as its shape, size, strength, and flexibility.

2. Select one item from your materials, for example an egg carton. Talk about how it was designed for a specific purpose—to keep eggs from touching and breaking. Brainstorm together new and creative uses for the carton. Do this with several different materials. Be creative and open to all suggestions.

3. What would your child like to build? Ideas might include a fire truck, a boat, a house, or a garage for a toy. Possibilities are unlimited!

4. Take time to explore the materials and test some ideas. When your child has an idea of what he wants to build, talk about and collect the necessary materials.

   ▸ *Do we have enough lids to use for tires?*

   ▸ *What will work for a sail? How can we attach it to the boat?*

   ▸ *How about trying paper towel tubes instead of these shorter tubes?*

   ▸ *Why did you choose this material to build your ____?*

5. Help as needed on the project. Encourage your child to do most of the material selection, connecting of materials, and construction. Work together to solve any construction problems.

6. If you have room, let your child take several days to work on an idea.

Aluminum Foil Boats

Make boats from aluminum foil, and experiment with how to make them float and carry objects.

Great Books to Read Before Doing This Activity

Boats by Anne Rockwell

Mr. Gumpy's Outing by John Burningham

Who Sank the Boat? by Pamela Allen

What's Needed

objects to be used as "passengers" or cargo in the boats, such as small
plastic blocks, washers, or pennies

pieces of aluminum foil: 6" x 6" squares work well, but any size and shape can be used

tub or pan of water

How to Do It

1. Talk with your child about what the word *sink* means. What might make a boat sink?

2. Show your child a flat sheet of foil and a small toy. Talk about how you might make the foil into a boat so that the toy can ride in it.

3. Create several boats, experimenting with different designs and testing each boat in the tub of water. Add animals or other toys to see what happens.

4. Talk about your boats and what you noticed when you put "passengers" in each boat. Does it make a difference where you put the passengers? Can some boats carry more passengers than others? Does the shape or size of the boat make a difference?

5. Test your ideas about boat designs by redesigning and floating many different boats.

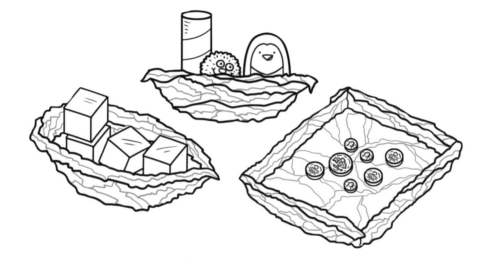

Paper Gliders

Experiment with paper airplane designs, and learn about air currents and how planes glide through the air.

Great Books to Read Before Doing This Activity

The Glorious Flight by Alice and Martin Provensen
Kids' Paper Airplane Book by Ken Blackburn
Nobody Owns the Sky by Reeve Lindbergh

What's Needed

a few pieces of 8½" x 11" paper
paper clips
scissors
tape

How to Do It

1. Fold a piece of paper in half the long way, and reopen it having the crease down the middle.

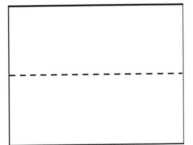

2. With the paper open, fold down two corners on the same short edge so that the corners and inside edges meet the fold and form two triangles.

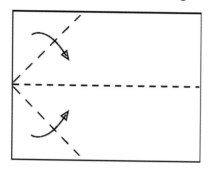

3. Starting with the outside points of the folded triangles, fold down the points so that the point and inside edges meet the fold.

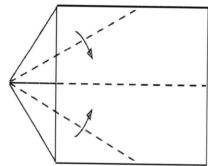

4. Turn the airplane over and fold the plane in half along the original crease.

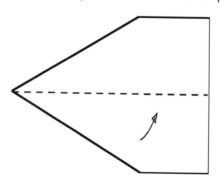

5. Taking the top straight edge, fold the diagonal edge down until it lines up with the original fold.

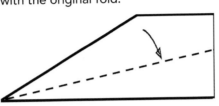

6. Turn the airplane over, and repeat step 5 so that it is even with the other side.

7. Straighten the wings to form the final shape.

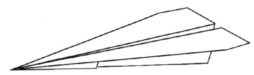

8. Launch the glider gently. See how it flies. Put a piece of tape across the wings to hold them together. Shape the wings so they have a slight upward curve. How does it fly now? See if you can make other changes to its flight.

9. For an additional challenge, design your own paper airplane gliders! Encourage your child to make a glider of his own design and then tell you how to build it, step by step.

10. Try different designs. Visit your local library or bookstore for books about paper airplanes. Search the Internet for more paper airplane designs.

Build a Spiral Spinner!

Make a spinner out of paper, and observe how it moves through the air.

Great Books to Read Before Doing This Activity

Feel the Wind by Arthur Dorros
I Face the Wind by Vicki Cobb
The Wind Blew by Pat Hutchins

What's Needed

8" x 8" piece of paper
scissors
string
tape

How to Do It

1. On the piece of paper, draw an 8" diameter circle.

2. Start at one edge of the circle, and cut a spiral going in toward the center of the circle. The number of coils will vary depending on how thin or thick you make the spiral cut—feel free to experiment, or just make it about 1" thick.

3. At the center of the spiral, poke a hole. Tie a knot at one end of your string. Pull the other end through the hole in the spiral until the knot stops at the hole. This way you don't tie the spiral tightly to the string.

4. Hold the string and move your arm up and down. What does the spinner do? Is it the same each time you pull it up or down?

5. Hold the spinner near a heat vent, a fan, or anything that might be blowing air—what happens? Try various places around your home, inside and outside.

Make a Paper Octopus

Experiment with a design for a paper octopus, and notice how it floats and moves.

Great Books to Read Before Doing This Activity

Flip, Float, Fly: Seeds on the Move by JoAnn Early Macken
Folding for Fun by Didier Boursin
Like a Windy Day by Frank Asch

What's Needed

4" x 6" piece of paper or any size rectangular piece of paper

scissors

tape

fold

How to Do It

1. In a 4" x 6" piece of paper, make two folds on the long edge about an inch or a finger's width apart. Crease well.

2. Open the folds, and cut strips perpendicular to the folds, making sure each cut meets the edge of the first fold.

3. Wrap one end of the top (the folded edge) around in a circle to meet the other end and tape. The strips/arms should lie flat.

4. Hold the "octopus" up in the air and drop it. What happens? How does it fly or float? If it spins, does it always go in the same direction?

5. You and your child can experiment with number of arms or the paper size you start with. How does this change the octopus's flight?

2

Growing and Changing

Growing and Changing

Children are interested in how things grow and change partly because *they* are growing and changing, too.

I'm getting new sneakers because my feet are too big for my old ones.

When I was a baby, I slept in a crib. Now I have a big bed.

All living things grow and show signs of change. Kittens grow into cats; grass grows and has to be cut; and seedlings grow into mature plants. Changes happen because of natural causes, and people cause changes, too. People change food when they cook and eat it. People change the environment when they build roads, dams, and houses. People can change a sheep's fleece into yarn or can change a tree into paper.

Here are some examples of how you and your child can explore growth and change:

▸ Talk with your child about growth and the differences between being a baby and being a "big kid."

▸ Discuss how children and all people change as they grow older.

▸ Observe how seeds germinate and grow into plants.

▸ Observe and measure a plant as it grows.

▸ Observe life cycles of common animals.

▸ Observe and record changes in living material during decomposition.

▸ Observe and record changes in one tree and the environment around it over several seasons.

Collecting data and communicating this information helps you and your child think back on what you have observed, sorted, or measured. Drawings, charts, and graphs help her organize and understand information in a visual form. These visual representations help her tell others about what you have observed and explored. The investigations in this section provide many opportunities for collecting and representing data.

Books

Your public library or local bookstore will have lots of books about growth and change. Remember to look for nonfiction books as well as fiction. When you read nonfiction books with your child, keep in mind that these books are not meant to be read aloud from cover to cover. Read a nonfiction book over a few days or even a week, taking the time to look at the pictures and talk about what you see.

Here are just a few books about growing and changing that you and your child will enjoy:

Animal Growth

A New Frog by Pamela Hickman
Arabella Miller's Tiny Caterpillar by Clare Jarrett
Growing Like Me by Anne Rockwell
Monarch Butterfly by Gail Gibbons
Waiting for Wings by Lois Ehlert

Plant Growth

Be a Friend to Trees by Patricia Lauber
Flip, Float, Fly: Seeds on the Move by JoAnn Early Macken
From Seed to Plant by Gail Gibbons
How a Seed Grows by Helene Jordan
Jody's Beans by Malachy Doyle
A Log's Life by Wendy Pfeffer

I'm Growing and Changing

Make a book about how you have grown and changed.

Great Books to Read Before Doing This Activity
I'm Growing by Aliki
Now I'm Big by Margaret Miller
When Frank Was Four by Alison Lester

What's Needed
construction paper
crayons
markers
paper
photographs or drawings
stapler or hole punch
string or yarn
tape or glue

How to Do It
1. Have a conversation with your child about when she was a baby. What can you each remember? Talk about what she ate, liked to do, where she slept, and so on.

2. Using these ideas, create an *I'm Growing and Changing* book to record some of these changes. You can make a small book by folding blank sheets of paper in half and using a folded piece of construction paper for the cover.

3. Staple the folded edges together, or make small holes and use yarn or string to sew the pages and cover together.

4. Write, "When I was a baby, I…" on the left side of each page spread. On the right side write, "Now that I'm big, I…." Add your child's words to finish the sentences.

5. Your child can draw all the pictures, or she can use a mix of photographs and drawings.

6. Add to the book when you have time. Be sure to share the book with other family members and friends.

Measure Me!

Estimate your heights, then measure yourselves using a nonstandard unit and make comparisons.

Great Books to Read Before Doing This Activity
Actual Size by Steve Jenkins
How Big Is a Foot? by Rolf Myller
Twelve Snails to One Lizard by Susan Hightower

What's Needed
masking tape
nonstandard measuring unit, such as chopsticks (use large objects for younger children)

How to Do It
1. Ask your child to lie on the floor while you place pieces of masking tape to mark her head and feet. Then have your child stand up and see how long (tall) she is.

2. Hold up the object that will be used for measuring, such as a chopstick. Ask your child to estimate how many chopsticks will fit between the two pieces of tape on the floor.

3. Help your child place chopsticks end to end from one piece of tape to the other. Talk about how you are measuring how long she is with chopsticks. Encourage your child to help count the total number of chopsticks.

4. Now it is your child's turn! Ask your child to place pieces of tape near your head and near your feet while you lie on the floor. Lay chopsticks from end to end and count how many chopsticks tall you are.

5. Chart and compare the results. Who is the longest? How many chopsticks long?

6. Try smaller units of measure (such as clothespins) and measure again. Compare those results to the measurements you took with chopsticks. How do they compare? Can you think why they might be different?

7. You can also repeat this investigation as your child grows taller. Keep your original data so you can continue to make comparisons over time.

Estimating and Predicting

An *estimate* is an informed guess about quantities and measurements. We are estimating when we answer questions such as, *How many do you think we have? How far do you think we have to go? How cold do you think it is?* The more we practice estimating, the more we improve our skills of observation and spatial visualization.

Predictions do not always require quantities. Predictions can be about what we think is likely to happen. Here are some examples:

I predict the hawk will land on that tree because it is the tallest, and they like high places.

I think the sunset will be red and orange because it was like that yesterday.

As We Grow

Match and sort a collection of pictures of people of different ages.

Great Books to Read Before Doing This Activity

Growing Like Me by Anne Rockwell

Lots of Grandparents by Shelley Rotner

You'll Soon Grow into Them, Titch by Pat Hutchins

What's Needed

glue

magazines and catalogs with pictures of people of different ages—babies, children, and adults

(You may want to use some pictures of your own family.)

paper

scissors

How to Do It

1. Working together, build your collection of pictures by helping your child cut out pictures of people from magazines and catalogs. Be sure to include people of different ages.

2. Allow your child plenty of time to look at and talk about the various pictures. Talk about the age characteristics you notice. Do people of different ages do the same activities? What are the same? What are different?

3. What sorting groups can you and your child think of? Following are some sorting possibilities:

   ▶ *By age groups—babies, children, teenagers, and adults,*

   ▶ *By pairs of people about the same age*

   ▶ *By a sequence from youngest to oldest or oldest to youngest.*

4. Sort and re-sort your picture collection.

5. Make "As We Grow" time lines. Select sequences of pictures from the collection, and glue them onto a long strip of paper.

6.

Sprouting Seeds

Observe seeds and the conditions that are necessary for germination (sprouting).

Great Books to Read Before Doing This Activity

A Fruit Is a Suitcase for Seeds by Jean Richards
A Seed Is Sleepy by Dianna Hutts Aston
Seeds by Ken Robbins

What's Needed

bean seeds
magnifying glass
paper plates
paper towels
water

How to Do It

1. Working together, place several bean seeds between moist paper towels held between two plates (to preserve the moisture). Place the beans so they are not touching.

2. Place a few seeds on another plate, and keep these dry for comparison and discussion.

3. Ask your child to check the seeds daily to make sure the paper towels are still damp. In five to seven days, see which seeds have germinated.

4. Use your magnifying lens to observe the germinated seeds.

   ▸ *What do you notice about the germinated seeds?*

   ▸ *How are they the same and how are they different from the dry seeds?*

5. Help your child make a drawing comparing the germinated seeds to the dry seeds.

Sprouting Seeds Four Ways

What is the best way to sprout a seed? Experiment with germinating seeds under various conditions.

Great Books to Read Before Doing This Activity

From Seed to Plant by Allan Fowler
How a Seed Grows by Helene Jordan
One Bean by Anne Rockwell

What's Needed

bean seeds
bowl
magnifying glass
paper plates
paper towels
sunny spot near a window
water

How to Do It

1. Divide the bean seeds into four groups.

2. For the first group, repeat the paper-towel procedure used in Sprouting Seeds on page 42.

3. For the second group, presoak the bean seeds for 24 hours in water. Then follow the directions for germinating the seeds on paper towels as used in step 2.

4. For the third group, follow the directions in the Sprouting Seeds activity, but put the covered plates in bright, warm sunlight.

5. For the fourth group, follow the directions in the Sprouting Seeds activity, but place the seeds between dry paper towels.

6. Be sure to label each condition, and check every day to be sure the damp towels stay damp.

7. In one week's time, look at the seeds with a magnifier. Talk about your observations.

> *How many seeds germinated in each situation?*
> *How did the germination compare among the four experiments?*
> *What might be the reasons for the differences?*
> *What were the best growing conditions? Do you have an idea why?*

Facts About Plants

> Most plants need air, water, light, and food to live and grow.
> Most plants make seeds for new plants.
> Plants closely resemble their parents.
> Plants have life cycles that include being born, developing into adults, reproducing, and eventually dying and decomposing. Life cycles can look different for different plants.
> Many foods we eat are seeds, such as beans, rice, corn, and wheat.
> A *habitat* is the local environment in which a specific organism or species lives (pond, forest, ocean, and so forth).
> The *environment* is the natural world in which people, plants, and animals live.

Watch It Grow!

Plant seeds and study the changes as they sprout and grow.

Great Books to Read Before Doing This Activity

The Carrot Seed by Ruth Krauss

From Seed to Plant by Gail Gibbons

Roots, Shoots, Buckets, & Boots by Sharon Lovejoy

What's Needed

bean seeds

magnifying glass

marker

paper (for drawings)

pots or cups (with drain holes)

potting or garden soil

ruler

spoon or scoop

tape

water

yarn or string

How to Do It

1. Using a large spoon, help your child fill three pots or cups with soil.

2. Help him plant two or three bean seeds about 1" below the surface of the soil in each pot.

3. Water the seeds well in one of the pots. Put this pot in a bright indoor place. Keep the soil moist but not too wet. (Label this pot *SUN*.)

4. Add no water to one of the pots. Put this pot in a bright indoor place. (Label this pot *NO WATER*.)

5. Water one of the pots, and put it in a dark closet or cupboard. Keep the soil moist but not too wet. (Label this pot *NO SUN*.)

6. Your child should look at the pots every couple of days to watch for the seeds to sprout. As the seeds sprout and the plants grow, talk about what you see and about what plants need in order to grow.

   ▶ *How many leaves are there?*

   ▶ *What else do you notice? What has changed since the last time we looked?*

   ▶ *What do you notice about the seeds with no water?*

   ▶ *What do you notice about the seeds without light?*

7. Use a piece of yarn or string to measure one of your plants as it grows. On a large piece of paper, draw a line at the bottom representing the top level of the soil the plants are growing in. Each time you measure, tape the cut piece of yarn or string vertically with one end at the line. Mark the date at the bottom of each measurement.

Root Viewer

With this root viewer you can observe the development of roots in a growing plant.

Great Books to Read Before Doing This Activity

How a Seed Grows by Helene Jordan
Tops and Bottoms by Janet Stevens
What Do Roots Do? by Kathleen V. Kudlinski

What's Needed

bean seeds
clear (transparent) plastic cup
magnifying glass
markers or crayons
paper
paper towels
water

How to Do It

1. Dampen one or two sections of paper towel. Put the damp paper towel in the clear cup so it touches the sides and bottom.

2. Place several seeds about halfway down the cup, so the seeds are between the paper towel and the side of the cup. You should see the seeds from the outside.

3. Put the cup in a place where you and your child can see it. Be sure to keep the paper towel moist.

4. Watch the cup for several days. When the seeds sprout, use the magnifying glass to look closely at the root systems. What details do you notice?

5. Together, you can make drawings of the sprouting seeds or just talk about how they're changing.

Let Your Garden Grow!

Plant a small flower or vegetable garden at your home or find a place in your town where you could help grow some plants.

In your yard or at a park, look carefully at as many different plants as you can find. What similarities do you notice? What differences do you see? Can you name any of the plants?

Decomposition Conditions

Experiment with speeding up and slowing down decomposition.

Great Books to Read Before Doing This Activity

Garbage Helps Our Garden Grow by Linda Glaser
A Log's Life by Wendy Pfeffer
The Magic School Bus Meets the Rot Squad by Joanna Cole

What's Needed

camera (optional)
magnifying glass
plate
refrigerator
small pumpkin

How to Do It

1. For another challenge, follow the same procedures as in The Icky Factor: Decomposition on page 50, except place one of the chunks of pumpkin shell in a cold spot (such as the refrigerator) and another in a warm spot (such as on a counter or windowsill).

2. Observe and compare the decomposition of the pumpkin in cold and warm temperatures. Which shell decomposes faster? Why do you think this is so?

3. Over a period of several weeks, look at and talk about the changes you notice.

Decomposition: Plants at the End of Their Life Cycles

Plants need water, air, and nutrients in order to grow. When they die, the plant parts change back to what they took from the soil and air as they decay. *Decomposition* is the term for this very complicated and busy process. Because of the "icky" factor, children seldom get a chance to explore this important part of growing and changing. Decomposition is a process necessary for the continuation of life, since it creates essential nutrients that plants and animals need and use.

Getting to Know a Tree

Find a tree to visit and observe, and document how it and the environment around it change over time.

Great Books to Read Before Doing This Activity
Be a Friend to Trees by Patricia Lauber
Tell Me, Tree: All About Trees for Kids by Gail Gibbons
We Planted a Tree by Diane Muldrow

What's Needed
a tree that you can visit regularly
camera
hole punch
magnifying glass
markers or crayons
measuring tools
paper
string or yarn

How to Do It
1. Locate a tree in your yard, your neighborhood, or a local park that will be easy to visit monthly.
2. On your first visit, observe your tree carefully. Talk with your child, and collect information about what you notice.

    ▸ *What do you see in the tree?*

    ▸ *What do you observe under the tree?*

    ▸ *What colors do you see? What shapes?*

    ▸ *What special smells do you notice? Can you describe the smells?*

> ▸ *Stand quietly and listen. What do you hear?*
>
> ▸ *Touch the tree. Describe what you feel.*
>
> ▸ *Look at the tree and the surrounding area with a magnifying glass.*
>
> ▸ *Measure the tree. Use a piece of string or a measuring tape.*
>
> ▸ *Try to collect a leaf.*

3. Look carefully for signs of animal life in and around the tree. You might see squirrels, leaves chewed by insects, or birds' nests. From a short distance away, sit and watch the tree quietly. Are there any birds or animals visiting the tree?

4. Make a drawing of the tree. If possible, take a photograph of the tree.

5. When you return home, write on a piece of paper, *Our First Visit to Our Tree*, and the month. Make a record of your observations, including what you saw in and around the tree, what you heard and smelled, and any other information about your tree including your drawings, photographs, and a leaf.

6. Talk about the changes you might see on your next visit.

7. In one month, visit the tree again. Repeat your investigation, and record your data on a new page when you return home. You may want to add new categories to your record, including *Changes We Noticed*.

8. Staple your second page to the first one, or punch holes along the left side of the papers, and tie them together with string or yarn to make a book.

9. Visit your tree once a month for several seasons or a year. Continue to collect your data, make comparisons, and compile drawings and photographs in your book.

3

Out and About

Out and About

Why Should Children Learn about the Natural World?

Children love to explore the outdoors. When children splash around in puddles, make shadows, or watch the clouds change overhead, they are developing an awareness of their physical environment.

We all experience the wind, clouds, and rain; the sun and moon; the cycles of days, months, and seasons. By observing weather and cycles, we can notice how things change over time. A cycle is like a turning wheel. It turns around and around, with its parts in the same order, again and again. Day and night, the phases of the moon, and life cycles of living things are other examples of cycles. The concept of cycles is very important in science education.

You do not have to know the names of everything your child notices, nor do you need to answer every question! It is much more important to encourage a sense of curiosity and wonder than to provide facts your child may have difficulty remembering.

Your attitude has an influence on your child's learning. If you enjoy observing and exploring, your child will, too. Accepting his ideas about his discoveries is very important and is a great way to begin a conversation about further discoveries.

By reading about and exploring the world around you, you will be helping your child gain many different skills, for example:

- ▸ Noticing patterns
- ▸ Predicting possible outcomes based on observation and experience
- ▸ Observing changes over time
- ▸ Using the senses
- ▸ Collecting, recording, and representing discoveries and data in pictures, stories, and graphs

Books

Here are some book recommendations for talking about the natural world and outdoor experiences, weather, and shadows. Your public library or local bookstore will have many others to choose from. Look for books featuring characters that will help your child see the world in unique and special ways.

Come on, Rain by Karen Hesse

Down Comes the Rain by Franklyn Branley

Every Autumn Comes the Bear by Jim Arnosky

Heat Wave by Eileen Spinelli

Moonbear's Shadow by Frank Asch

Our Seasons by Ranida McKneally and Grace Lin

Phases of the Moon by Gillia Olson

Red Leaf, Yellow Leaf by Lois Ehlert

Weather Words and What They Mean by Gail Gibbons

Sound Walk

Listen closely to sounds in your everyday environment. What can you hear?

Great Books to Read Before Doing This Activity

Hello Ocean by Pam Munoz Ryan

Max Found Two Sticks by Brian Pinkney

Moses Goes to a Concert by Isaac Millman

What's Needed

A walking route!

How to Do It

1. Start indoors: Sit with your child very quietly, cupping your hands behind your ears in order to focus more closely. What do you hear?

2. With your child's help, write down all of the sounds you hear, and describe what each sound is, for example, "The clock *tick-tocked*," "The telephone rang," and so on. Call this list *Indoor Sounds*.

3. Go for an outdoor sound walk with your child. As you walk, stop every few minutes and be quiet together, cupping your hands behind your ears and listening to sounds. Talk about everything you hear.

4. When you get home, make a list of the outdoor sounds you heard. Describe each sound: "The bus sounded like a big growl"; "A tree is very quiet, but you can hear the wind rustling its leaves." Call this list *Outdoor Sounds.*

5. Make your two sound lists into two books. Your child can illustrate the sounds in each book, and he can share the book with family and friends.

Make a Wind Flag

Make a tool to use as you explore and investigate wind and air movement.

Great Books to Read Before Doing This Activity

Feel the Wind by Arthur Dorros
I Face the Wind by Vicki Cobb
The Wind Blew by Pat Hutchins

What's Needed

fabric paint (optional)
glue or tape
one stick or dowel, approximately 2' long
permanent markers (optional)
pieces of nylon material cut into long rectangles or triangles (an old pillowcase works, too!)
twine or yarn

How to Do It

1. Talk about the wind: *How do we know when the wind is blowing?* (A waving flag, bad hairdos, laundry flapping on a clothesline, leaves shaking on a tree).

2. What words do we use to describe the wind blowing? (If your child cannot think of any words, ask him to imitate the sound the wind makes: *Whoosh!*)

3. Choose the material you want to use to make your wind flag. Your child might want to decorate the material with fabric paint or permanent markers. Thread a 2' piece of dowel or stick through small holes cut into each side of the fabric, or tie a length of twine through each hole onto the dowel.

4. Experiment inside first and ask your child to move the flag around to observe what happens to it.

5. Go outside to discover which direction the wind is blowing. First, find a place outside where you can feel a breeze, then find a place where you are protected from the wind.

6. On another day, visit the same places outside to see if the wind has changed direction or if it is windy at all.

Tracking Air Currents with Bubbles

Use soap bubbles to follow how air moves around outside.

Great Books to Read Before Doing This Activity

Air Is All Around You by Franklyn Branley

Bubble Trouble by Margaret Mahy

Pop! A Book about Bubbles by Kimberley Brubaker Bradley

What's Needed

bucket

dishwashing liquid

measuring cup

plastic drinking straws

scissors

string

water

How to Do It

1. Mix 11 cups of water with one cup of dishwashing liquid in a bucket to make a bubble solution.

2. Cut a straw in half, and cut a piece of string 18 to 20 inches long.

3. Feed the string through the two straw halves and tie the string into a loop.

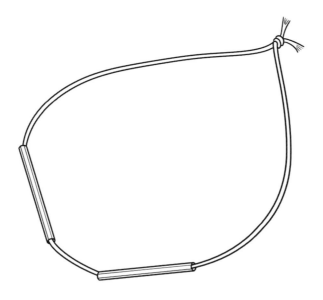

4. Hold the straws together like a handle (tape them together if you want), then dip the string loop into your soap solution and pull it out.

5. Gently wave the loop around, creating a bubble. You should be able to get a bubble off the loop and into the air after some practice.

6. Make a lot of bubbles outside your home. Watch and follow the bubbles as they move toward and away from your home. The bubbles will show you the air currents. *Do you notice any patterns? Which way is the air moving?*

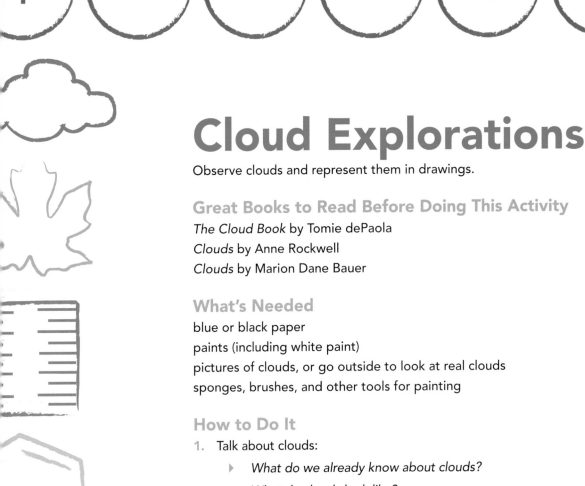

Cloud Explorations

Observe clouds and represent them in drawings.

Great Books to Read Before Doing This Activity

The Cloud Book by Tomie dePaola
Clouds by Anne Rockwell
Clouds by Marion Dane Bauer

What's Needed

blue or black paper
paints (including white paint)
pictures of clouds, or go outside to look at real clouds
sponges, brushes, and other tools for painting

How to Do It

1. Talk about clouds:

   ▶ *What do we already know about clouds?*

   ▶ *What do clouds look like?*

   ▶ *What are clouds made from?*

   ▶ *Do they move?*

   ▶ *What can fall to earth from them?*

   ▶ *What colors can clouds be?*

2. Using books or pictures, introduce the idea that clouds create different patterns and have different shapes. Observe and talk about the cloud patterns in the sky or in your pictures.

3. Ask your child what words she would use to describe the clouds, and make a list of those words.

4. Get out the art supplies and invite your child to make cloud prints or paintings to record the kinds of clouds you have seen. Use brushes, sponges, or different tools to create various patterns.

5. Share your cloud paintings with your friends and family.

Puddles, Puddles

Observe puddles as they change over time, appearing and disappearing (evaporating).

Great Books to Read Before Doing This Activity
Down Comes the Rain by Franklyn Branley
Puddles by Jonathan London
Where Do Puddles Go? by Fay Robinson

What's Needed
chalk or string
container for water
puddles from a recent rainstorm (or made with water from your garden hose)

How to Do It
1. Talk about where you have seen puddles form when it rains. Are there places nearby where you might find puddles?
2. After a rainstorm, find an area with puddles on concrete or blacktop. If you live in an area where it seldom rains, make your own puddle with water from a garden hose.
3. Trace around the puddle with chalk, or lay out string around the edge. Leave the puddle for a while.
4. Return to check on the puddle after a few hours. What has happened? Encourage your child to trace around the puddle again or move the string. What are some of your child's ideas about what has happened to the water?
5. Try to observe the puddle a couple of times before it has totally evaporated.

6. Make puddles again on a hot day, and see how fast they evaporate (change from a liquid to a vapor).

7. Puddles indoors: If you do not have an outside area to make puddles, you can make puddles inside! Fill two shallow containers with water. Cover one container with a lid or a plastic bag.

8. Put both containers in a sunny location. Observe the containers over time, and talk about changes that you see. *What happens to the water in the container with the lid? What happens to the water in the uncovered container?*

The Water Cycle

Water in a puddle or dish evaporates into the air, and the heat of the sun speeds this process. A cover on a container stops the water vapor from leaving, so water droplets collect on the cover and fall back into the dish. In the natural cycle, water evaporates and joins the moisture in the air, becoming clouds. Eventually, it becomes rain or other forms of precipitation.

Where Did the Water Come From?

Pull water out of thin air by creating condensation.

Great Books to Read Before Doing This Activity

Come on, Rain by Karen Hesse
Down Comes the Rain by Franklyn Branley
A Drop around the World by Barbara Shaw McKinney

What's Needed

cover for your pitcher or jar
ice cubes
pitcher or large jar
very cold water

How to Do It

1. Together, put the ice cubes into the pitcher of water.

2. Observe and talk about what is happening on the outside of the pitcher. What do you see?

3. Where did the droplets of water come from? If you place a lid on the jar, will the droplets continue to form?

4. What is happening? When air is cooled it cannot hold as much moisture as when air is warm. When warm air comes into contact with the cold jar, the air cools off, and the moisture it was holding is released in the form of droplets, called *condensation*.

Make It Rain!

Use simple tools to try making rain!

Great Books to Read Before Doing This Activity

Come on, Rain by Karen Hesse
Down Comes the Rain by Franklyn Branley
In the Rain with Baby Duck by Amy Hest

What's Needed

clear glass or plastic container
hot water (adult only)
ice cubes
paper
pencil
plate

How to Do It

1. Talk with your child about where rain might come from. Make a list of your ideas.
2. Fill your container with very hot tap water.
3. Place the plate on top of the container.
4. After a few minutes, place ice cubes on top of the plate.
5. Look through the side of the container, and notice what happens. This is similar to what happens outdoors as warm, moist air rises and meets colder temperatures. Water vapor condenses and forms precipitation that falls to the earth as rain (or snow, sleet, or hail).

Measuring Temperature

Use a thermometer and begin to understand how to measure temperature.

Great Books to Read Before Doing This Activity

Heat Wave by Eileen Spinelli
One Hot Summer Day by Nina Crews
Snow by Uri Shulevitz

What's Needed

cold water
thermometer (one with alcohol liquid inside)
two cups
warm (not hot) water

How to Do It

1. Talk about how we know if it is hot or cold outside. What clues or observations do we use to decide? How can we measure the temperature of air more precisely?

2. Look at your thermometer, and talk about where the red line ends. Practice reading the numbers on the thermometer. The number where the red line ends tells us the temperature of the room. Thermometers work because the liquid in the tube expands as it warms and contracts when cooled.

3. Try placing your fingers or hands on the red bulb at the bottom of the thermometer. Ask the following questions:

    ▸ *What do you notice? What happens to the red line? Why do you think the red line got longer?*

    ▸ *Can you read the number where the red line ends?* That is the temperature of your body.

4. Ask your child to make some predictions: *What do you think will happen if we put the thermometer in a cup of cold water? in a cup of warm water?*
5. Help your child place the thermometer in the cold water, and observe the change in the red line. *Can you read the temperature of the cold water? Is it higher or lower than the temperature of the room?*
6. Now place the thermometer in the warm water, and observe the change in the red line. *Can you read the temperature of the warm water? Is it higher or lower than the temperature of the room?*

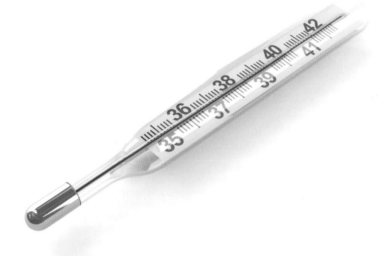

Make a Rain Gauge

Create a tool to measure the amount of rain that falls.

Great Books to Read Before Doing This Activity
Come on, Rain by Karen Hesse
Red Rubber Boot Day by Mary Lyn Ray
Who Likes Rain? by Wong Herbert Yee

What's Needed
clear jar with straight sides, like an olive jar
paper or notebook
pencil
ruler

How to Do It

1. Place the jar outside in an open area (not too close to buildings or under trees) before it starts to rain.

2. After the rain has fallen, check your jar. Is there water in it?

3. Use your ruler to measure how much rain has been collected in your jar.

4. Together, record the date and how much rain you collected.

5. Empty the jar after each use.

That's Some Wild Weather We're Havin'!

We live on a planet that is surrounded by a thin layer of gases called the *atmosphere*. Weather is the set of conditions occurring at any single moment and location within the atmosphere. It is measured in terms of such things as wind direction and speed, temperature, humidity, atmospheric pressure, cloudiness, and precipitation. In most places, weather can change from hour to hour, day to day, and season to season.

Creating a Weather Chart

Observe, record, and measure the weather, noticing patterns and making predictions.

Great Books to Read Before Doing This Activity

On the Same Day in March by Marilyn Singer
Weather Forecasting by Gail Gibbons
Weather Words and What They Mean by Gail Gibbons

What's Needed

calendar pages with large squares
outdoor thermometer
pencil
rain gauge from Make a Rain Gauge, page 74

How to Do It

1. Set up an outdoor thermometer to record temperatures.

2. Use the rain gauge you used in the Make a Rain Gauge activity to measure rainfall.

3. Talk about words used to describe weather: *hot, cold, sunny, rainy, humid, cloudy, stormy, thundering, snowing, foggy, windy.*

4. Help your child make a monthly weather calendar. Put your calendar in a convenient place.

5. In each date square, record observations, temperature, and rainfall. Talk about how the weather today is the same or different from the weather yesterday or last week.

6. Get the whole family involved in recording the daily weather. Do not worry if you have to skip days; you will still be able to make comparisons and notice similarities and differences in weather patterns.

August

Sunday	Monday	Tuesday	Wednesday	Thursday	Friday	Saturday
			1 cool and rainy 60° 2" rain	2 windy and rainy 55° 1" rain	3 cold and cloudy 50°	4 cold and cloudy 35°
5 very cold and rainy 28 1" rain	6	7 windy and very cold 22	8 snow is falling! 17 3" snow	9 cold and more snow! 18° 1" snow	10	11
12	13	14	15	16	17	18
19	20	21	22	23	24	25

Weather Patterns

Use your weather chart to recognize weather patterns over time.

Great Books to Read Before Doing This Activity
Clouds by Anne Rockwell
Come on, Rain by Karen Hesse
Weather Forecasting by Gail Gibbons

What's Needed
outdoor thermometer
rain gauge from Make a Rain Gauge, page 74
weather chart from Creating a Weather Chart, page 76

How to Do It
1. Set up an outdoor thermometer to record temperatures.
2. Use the rain gauge you made in the Make a Rain Gauge activity to measure rainfall.
3. Using your weather chart, record observations, temperature, and rainfall. Talk about how the weather today is the same or different from the weather yesterday or last week.
4. Discuss and list interesting observations that can be collected about your local weather: *Are there snowstorms or thunderstorms where you live? Is it foggy in the morning and sunny in the afternoon?* As you collect information, there will be many opportunities to look for patterns and to make comparisons and predictions.

5. At the end of the month, look at and talk about your chart. Use your weather data for counting and comparing questions such as:

    ▸   *How many sunny days did we have this week?*

    ▸   *How many inches of rain fell in that last storm?*

    ▸   *What do you notice about the temperature?*

    ▸   *What do you notice about the rainfall?*

    ▸   *What was the coldest temperature?*

    ▸   *What was the warmest temperature?*

6. Save data for several months to make comparisons: *Which month(s) had the most rainy days? the most sunny days? the coldest temperatures? the warmest temperatures?*

Outside Shadows

Play with your shadows and see what you observe.

Great Books to Read Before Doing This Activity

Moonbear's Shadow by Frank Asch
Nothing Sticks Like a Shadow by Ann Tompert
What Makes a Shadow? by Clyde Robert Bulla

What's Needed

several large, lightweight objects to take outdoors, such as an umbrella, a broom, a hoop, or a jump rope
sunny day

How to Do It

1. On a sunny day, talk about investigating shadows outside.

2. Go outside and make a variety of shadows with your bodies or with the objects you have brought outside.

3. Talk about the shadows. *What do they look like? How does the shadow differ from the object causing the shadow?*

4. Some ideas to try:

   ▸ *Can you make your shadows smaller?*

   ▸ *Can you make your shadows bigger?*

   ▸ Make your shadows touch even though you and your child are not touching each other.

   ▸ Try to hide your shadow.

You and your child will have other ideas to try once you begin playing with shadows.

5. Experiment with different objects outside that will make interesting shadows. Make as many different shadows as you can.

Growing and Shrinking Shadow

Observe how your shadow moves and how it changes size over the course of a day.

Great Books to Read Before Doing This Activity

Moonbear's Shadow by Frank Asch
Shadows by April Pulley Sayre
Shadows and Reflections by Tana Hoban

What's Needed

stick or chalk
stones
sunny day

How to Do It

1. Find a sunny place on the grass, dirt, or sidewalk.

2. Use a stick or chalk to mark where your child's toes are, so that he can stand in the exact same place later on.

3. While your child is standing in the marked location, place a stone on the ground on the shadow of his head.

4. Return to the same location in about an hour.

5. Help your child put his toes at the place you marked.

6. Now place a stone on the shadow of your child's head. *What has changed?*

7. Repeat this several times throughout the day, each time placing a new stone where the shadow of your child's head is. *What pattern do the stones make at the end of the day?*

Inside Shadows

Explore how light can create different sizes and shapes of shadows inside, using a flashlight.

Great Books to Read Before Doing This Activity

Shadow by Suzy Lee
Shadows and Reflections by Tana Hoban
Whose Shadow Is This? by Claire Berge

What's Needed

crayons or markers (to draw shadow patterns)
flashlight
paper
pen or marker
plastic toy animals, small stuffed animals, or other toys (at least 3" or 4" tall)

How to Do It

1. Place one of your small objects on a piece of paper on a table.
2. Turn on the flashlight, and make a shadow of the object on the paper.
3. Draw the outline of the shadow on the paper with your pen or marker.
4. Move the light, and see what happens to the shadow. Move the flashlight several times. Each time make a drawing of the new shadow on the same piece of paper. *Can you make a long shadow? a short shadow? Is the shadow always the same shape as the object?*
5. Try using different objects to make shadows.
6. *Can you make the shadow of an object smaller than the actual object? Can you make it bigger?*

Make Your Own Sun

Use a flashlight to imitate our experience of the sun traveling across the sky each day.

Great Books to Read Before Doing This Activity

The Sun: Our Nearest Star by Franklyn Branley
Sun Up, Sun Down by Gail Gibbons
Sun Up, Sun Down: The Story of Day and Night by Jacqui Bailey

What's Needed

flashlight
paper
plastic toy animals, small stuffed animals, or other toys (at least 3" or 4" tall)

How to Do It

1. Pretend the flashlight is the sun, and use it to make a shadow of an object on the paper.

2. Move your "sun" slowly clockwise in a curved path around your object, imitating what we experience as the sun's daily motion of rising in the east and setting in the west. *How do the shadows change? When are they longest? When are they shortest?*

4

Investigating Animals and Insects

Investigating Animals and Insects

Children are fascinated by animals and insects! They have endless questions: *What is that? What does it eat? Where does it live? How does it move? What sound does it make?* You can help your child learn about, care for, and respect nature if you enjoy exploring and interacting with other living things together. Through these positive experiences, your child will begin to learn that people have a role in caring for the other living things that share the environment with us.

Through direct experience and observation, your child can learn that a habitat is a home place. It is an area that provides everything a plant or animal needs to survive—food, water, air, shelter, and space. Our homes are our habitats the way a rotting log is the habitat for ants. The plants and animals that live in a particular habitat are suited to that place. A fish could not live in a field, and a mouse could not live in an ocean. You do not need a forest to teach your child about the environment. A schoolyard or park—even your own backyard!—is an appropriate starting place. What is important is that every habitat is special because it is home to a wonderful variety of living things.

Far More than Fiction

In addition to using picture books to introduce a science topic, you may want to look at and read nonfiction books about that topic. For instance, you could pair a story such as Chris Van Allsburg's *Two Bad Ants* with a good nonfiction book about ants.

Nonfiction books present facts and photographs or drawings about a subject. Consider the following when reading and looking at nonfiction books with your child:

▶ Nonfiction books are not meant to be read out loud with a child from cover to cover. However, before you read a nonfiction book with your child, do as you would with a picture book, and read it yourself from cover to cover.

▶ Choose the parts of the book that reinforce, extend, or otherwise add to the concept you are exploring with your child.

▶ Give your child time to look closely at photographs and illustrations. Read the captions out loud.

▶ Stop reading after a few facts, and talk about them.

▶ Talk about the differences between the picture book and the nonfiction book. *Do the ants in the photo look like the two bad ants? How are they the same? How are they different?*

There are many wonderful picture books and nonfiction titles about all kinds of animals. Here are just a few examples:

Arabella Miller's Tiny Caterpillar by Clare Jarrett

Birds by Kevin Henkes

Bugs Are Insects by Anne Rockwell

In the Tall, Tall Grass by Denise Fleming

A Log's Life by Wendy Pfeffer

Monarch Butterfly by Gail Gibbons

Mouse Views by Bruce McMillan

Seashells by the Seashore by Marianne Berkes

Two Bad Ants by Chris Van Allsburg

What Do You Do with a Tail Like This? by Steve Jenkins

My Own Nature Journal

Use drawings, photographs, writing, and objects you collect to tell others about what you learn and discover.

Great Books to Read Before Doing This Activity

A Desert Scrapbook by Virginia Wright-Frierson
Diary of a Pet Turkey by Joanne Ingis
Diary of a Worm by Doreen Cronin

What's Needed

camera (optional)
notebook or paper
writing and drawing tools (paints, crayons, markers, and so on)

How to Do It

1. A nature journal is a record of outdoor experiences that contains details of your observations and activities. A nature journal can include many kinds of records: You can write, draw pictures with crayons or markers, record sounds with a tape recorder, or take photos with a camera, to name just a few. Here are some ideas you might want to try:

   ▸ Take photos and have your child dictate captions.

   ▸ Encourage your child to draw pictures and dictate sentences to describe a discovery or event.

   ▸ Use *all* of your senses, so you can describe smells, sounds, textures, and so on.

- Create a list of questions and predictions to explore.
- Create charts and graphs of the details you notice and the measurements you make.
- Describe your feelings about what you see and do.
- Add samples of flowers and leaves.

Journal data most often include the following:

- Date, time, and place;
- Weather conditions;
- Written descriptions of observations you made using your senses;
- Written reflections and comparisons containing personal feelings and opinions; and
- Labeled drawings or photos of what you have observed.

Find additional information at
http://familyfun.go.com/parenting/learn/activities/feature/famf78nature
   famf78nature.html

Getting to Know a Place

Develop looking, listening, and describing skills as you use different senses to explore areas outside.

Great Books to Read Before Doing This Activity

Backyard by Donald Silver
In the Small, Small Pond by Denise Fleming
In the Tall, Tall Grass by Denise Fleming

What's Needed

fabric bag (a pillowcase works well, too)
objects with different textures, such as sandpaper, cotton balls, and a small piece of plastic
paint-sample cards of many colors

How to Do It

I Spy

1. Play I Spy by describing an object that you can see. Give your child three or four clues of color, size, or location. After each clue, ask your child to try to guess the object. Continue offering clues until he discovers the object you have spied.

2. Switch roles. Ask your child to describe something he sees so you can guess what it might be. (Make sure not to guess it right away, even if you know the answer. Ask for a couple of hints.)

Color Search

1. Make a set of color cards by cutting up some paint-sample cards. (These are available for free at most home-improvement and hardware stores.) Choose a variety of colors.

2. Ask your child to choose one of the color cards, then try to find a color match with something outdoors. **Hint:** You may want to vary the color choices according to the season or the particular area you will be visiting. A collection of bright colors will work well in the summer in a garden, but a collection of shades of green will require looking carefully for small differences in grasses, leaves, or moss.

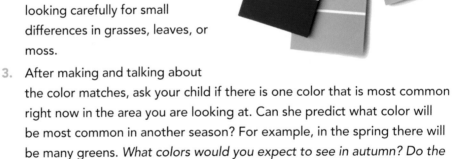

3. After making and talking about the color matches, ask your child if there is one color that is most common right now in the area you are looking at. Can she predict what color will be most common in another season? For example, in the spring there will be many greens. *What colors would you expect to see in autumn? Do the colors change seasonally where you live?*

Sounds Around

1. Find a comfortable place to sit outside. You are going to practice listening like a rabbit to the sounds around you. Cup your hands behind your ears to make rabbit ears.

2. Sit quietly together for a few minutes and listen to the sounds around you. You might suggest that your child close her eyes while listening.

3. Talk about and make a list of the sounds you heard. *Did you hear natural sounds like the wind or water? Did you hear sounds made by people or machines?*

4. Try listening at another location and collecting more descriptions of sounds. Talk with your child about what is alike and what is different between the sounds at the different locations.

Feeling Textures

1. Collect a few objects with different textures. Some examples could be sandpaper, a cotton ball, and a piece of smooth plastic.

2. Put one of the objects in a bag so it cannot be seen. Ask your child to reach into the bag and feel the texture of the object.

3. Now, ask your child to look for something in the habitat that has the same texture as the object in the bag. Can she find more than one thing? Encourage your child to compare the textures of the objects she finds.

4. Repeat this with another texture.

Our Own Backyard

Explore a small area of ground, observing and recording what you see.

Great Books to Read Before Doing This Activity

Backyard by Donald Silver
In the Tall, Tall Grass by Denise Fleming
On Meadowview Street by Henry Cole

What's Needed

magnifying glass (optional)
nature journal from My Own Nature Journal, page 91
pencil or crayon
two 3'–5' foot lengths of string or yarn

How to Do It

1. Go outside to a place where you and your child can safely crawl on the ground and explore.

2. Make a yarn or string loop on the grass, one for each of you. These will define areas to explore.

3. Get down on the ground, and explore your areas. Take your time. If you have them, use magnifying glasses or other magnifiers to look even more closely.

4. Talk about what is inside your loops:

    ▸ *What do you see in the grass?*

    ▸ *How many different creatures do you find?*

    ▸ *What does the grass look like up close?*

    ▸ *How might it feel to be as small as an insect?*

5. Record your exploration by drawing pictures of some of the things you see in your nature journal.

6. Your child can tell you about the area, and you can write down the names, colors, and descriptions of what he has seen.

Make a Mini-Habitat

Create your own mini-environment, and watch it as it changes over time.

Great Books to Read Before Doing This Activity
In the Tall, Tall Grass by Denise Fleming
One Small Square: Woods by Donald Silver
The Kids' Nature Book by Susan Milford

What's Needed
container with a lid (a plastic salad or deli box works well)
plants such as grass or moss
seeds
small container of water for a pond
soil
spray bottle filled with water
sticks
stones

How to Do It
1. Gather the materials to use in your mini-habitat.
2. Help your child add the soil, seeds, and plants to the container.
3. Place sticks and stones around the plants wherever you think they should go.
4. Use a spray bottle of water to dampen the soil before closing the lid of the container.

5. Put the container in a spot where it will get bright, filtered light and where you and your child can see it easily. Keep it moist but not too wet.

6. Observe your mini-habitat for changes over time.

7. Draw pictures or tell stories about the changes you see.

A Collection of Natural Treasures

Build a collection of objects from nature to describe, compare, and classify.

Great Books to Read Before Doing This Activity

Let's Go Rock Collecting by Roma Gans
Rocks in His Head by Carol Otis Hurst
Seashells by the Seashore by Marianne Berkes

What's Needed

crayons or markers
an egg carton (or other container)
paper
scissors
tape or glue

How to Do It

1. Help your child make a special collection box from an egg carton. Cut a piece of paper to cover the writing on the lid. Your child can color and draw on this paper and write her name on it before taping or gluing it onto the carton.

2. Go on a walk to find natural treasures with which to start a collection. Your child might want to collect one type of thing, such as rocks, or different things, such as a feather, a pinecone, and a special leaf. Any kind of collection is okay, but discourage your child from collecting insects or other live creatures.

3. Bring the treasures inside, and ask your child to talk about one special treasure. *What makes this one special? Do you remember where you found it?*

4. Encourage your child to sort the collected objects into groups based on material, color, texture, or another feature.

5. For even more fun, challenge your child to go on a scavenger hunt with you to find items with specific characteristics. For example, try to find something round, something soft, or something green. Add these items to your collection of natural treasures.

Sorting Animals

Notice differences and similarities between and among animals, and then sort the pictures of the animals by the details you see.

Great Books to Read Before Doing This Activity

First Animal Encyclopedia by Penelope Arlon
I See a Kookaburra by Steve Jenkins
What Do You Do with a Tail Like This? by Steve Jenkins

What's Needed

a collection of pictures of animals, cut out from magazines or other sources

How to Do It

1. Look at and talk about the pictures of the animals. *What do you notice about the sizes of the animals? the colors? the number of legs? What else do you know about the various animals? What do they eat? How do they move? Where do they live?*

2. Sort the animals by some of the characteristics you have discussed: all the animals that have two legs, all the animals that have four legs, all the animals that fly, all the animals that live on a farm.

3. Use the animal pictures many times to sort and re-sort. Add to your collection of pictures!

Easy Sighting Scope

Create a "sighting scope" to look at familiar objects from a different perspective.

Great Books to Read Before Doing This Activity

Duck! Rabbit! by Amy Krouse Rosenthal
Mouse Views by Bruce McMillan
Two Bad Ants by Chris Van Allsburg

What's Needed

magnifying glass
paper towel tube

How to Do It

1. Place a small object on the floor.

2. Look at the object through the paper towel tube "sighting scope."

3. Look at the same object from different points around the room: Stand on a chair, lie on the floor and look across the room at it, and so on. *What is the same and what is different when you use the sighting scope? when you move around the room?*

4. Experiment with different objects, and take turns using your sighting scope to view the objects from different perspectives.

5. Now look at the same objects with a magnifying glass. *How do your observations differ from when you use the sighting scope?*

6. Help your child make drawings of her observations.

Which "Bug" Is Which?

Learn about the different features of insect and noninsect "bugs."

Great Books to Read Before Doing This Activity

The Best Book of Bugs by Claire Llewellyn
Bugs Are Insects by Anne Rockwell
Insects: Biggest! Littlest! by Sandra Markle

What's Needed

collection of insect and noninsect photographs, cut out from magazines or other sources

How to Do It

1. Gather a collection of insect and noninsect "bug" photographs. Look at the details of the photos.

2. Talk about the features of insects (see sidebar) and make comparisons with the features found in noninsect "bugs." As you look at each picture, ask these questions to guide your observations:

   ▸ *How many legs does this creature have?*

   ▸ *Does this bug have wings?*

   ▸ *How many body segments does this bug have?*

   ▸ *Does this bug have antennae?*

   ▸ *How many eyes does this creature have?*

3. Separate your collection of photos into two groups: insect and noninsect.

4. Try sorting your insect photos by a variety of characteristics, for example, by how they move (fly, walk, jump, burrow, and so on), by color, or by differences in the wings.

Is It an Insect?

Insects have these features:

▸ Three segmented body parts:

- The *head,* which may include one pair of antennae and one pair of compound eyes,

- The *thorax* with three pairs of legs and possibly two pairs of wings attached, and

- The *abdomen,* which contains numerous organs.

▸ An *exoskeleton* (a hard outside covering that has the muscles attached on the inside)

▸ *Bilateral symmetry* (the left and right sides of the body are mirror images of each other)

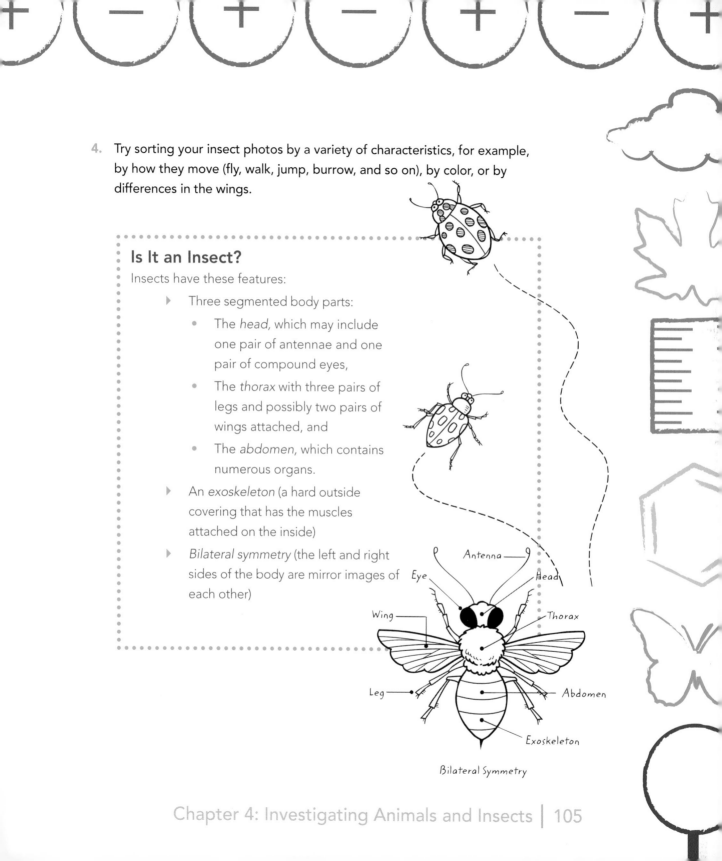

Antenna

Eye

Head

Wing

Thorax

Leg

Abdomen

Exoskeleton

Bilateral Symmetry

What Can We Learn about Spiders?

Learn about spiders by investigating their physical characteristics and making a model of a spider.

Great Books to Read Before Doing This Activity

Charlotte's Web by E. B. White (as a read aloud)
Spiders by Nic Bishop
Spinning Spiders by Melvin Berger

What's Needed

magnifying glass (optional)
materials for making a model: clay, chenille sticks, cotton balls, and so on
photograph of a spider

How to Do It

1. Talk about spiders. What does your child already know about them?

2. Find a photograph of a spider in a book or on the Internet. *Can you find the two main body parts? How many legs do you count? What does its head look like? How many eyes do you count?*

3. Take a walk outside and look for spiderwebs. Ask your child to look closely at a web. If possible, take a photograph of the web, especially if there is a spider present.

4. Encourage your child to build a model of a spider based on the photograph you first looked at and your observation of a spiderweb. If you saw a spider in the web, how was it the same and how was it different from the original photograph you looked at together?

Spider Facts

While we must be cautious with spiders (some have bites that can be poisonous), they are interesting creatures.

▶ A spider is not an insect. Spiders are called *arachnids*. Mites, ticks, and scorpions are also arachnids.

▶ Most spiders have eight legs, two body parts, and no wings or antennae.

▶ Spider legs are covered with tiny hairs.

▶ Most spiders have six or eight eyes.

▶ Spiders and insects are often seen together because most spiders feed on insects.

▶ Spiders use their mouthparts to inject poisons and paralyze their prey.

▶ Spiderwebs have fascinating structural designs and are incredibly strong.

▶ Different species of spiders weave different types of webs.

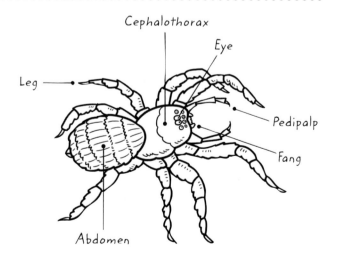

Cephalothorax

Eye

Leg

Pedipalp

Fang

Abdomen

Ant Hills and Sugar Trails

Use sugar to attract and observe ants or other insects on the sidewalk or in the yard.

Great Books to Read Before Doing This Activity

Ant Cities by Arthur Dorros
Are You an Ant? by Judy Allen
Two Bad Ants by Chris Van Allsburg

What's Needed

crayons or markers
magnifying glass
paper
small amount of sugar
sticks

How to Do It

1. Place small amounts of sugar in various spots around your yard or at the edge of a play area.

2. Put a stick in the ground next to each of your sugar hills so you can find them later.

3. Visit your sugar hills several times during the day and again the following day. Use a magnifying lens to get a better look at the insects that come to visit.

4. Encourage your child to make drawings of his observations. *What color were the ants he observed? How big were they? Did he notice any other insects that were attracted to the sugar?*

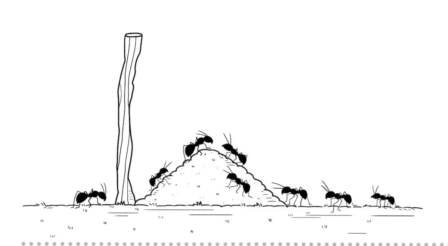

Here, Buggy-Buggy!

There are many ways to attract "bugs" for observation purposes:

▶ Place boards or flat stones on bare dirt and check underneath every day. Many bugs dislike openness where they are exposed to the drying sun and predators.

▶ Plant several kinds of ornamental flowering plants that provide pollen, nectar, fragrance, color, and shape.

▶ Place decomposing plant material in a hole dug into the dirt. Cover with an old plastic lid from a trash can, weighted down with a rock or a brick, so you can take a peek every day or two. This will attract a variety of bugs to observe.

▶ A small container (shallow enough so the insects will not drown) of sugar water will attract nectar feeders like honeybees and butterflies. A few slices of cut fruit will do the same.

Under the Rotting Log

There is a whole world of tiny living things we do not see very often. Investigating life under rocks and rotting logs lets us explore this hidden world.

Great Books to Read Before Doing This Activity

A Log's Life by Wendy Pfeffer
One Small Place in a Tree by Barbara Brenner
Under One Rock by Anthony Fredericks

What's Needed

Magnifying glass (optional)

How to Do It

1. Take a walk with your child, looking for rocks, rotting logs, even old scraps of wood around your yard or neighborhood.

2. Carefully pick up a rock or log, and quietly observe what you find underneath.

3. *How many different kinds of insects and other animals do you see?* Carefully watch what they are doing. *Are any carrying other insects, eggs, or objects?*

4. Gently put the rock or log back in its place. Try not to crush the insects you just observed.

5. Another time, look for rocks or logs in other locations. *Do you see the same insects or animals that you saw in your first exploration?*

6. Visit the same location once a week over a few months. *What changes have taken place each time?*

Caterpillar, What Will You Be?

Learn about the life cycle of a living thing by making models—begin with the caterpillar.

Great Books to Read Before Doing This Activity
Arabella Miller's Tiny Caterpillar by Clare Jarrett
Butterfly House by Eve Bunting
Monarch Butterfly by Gail Gibbons

What's Needed
chenille sticks (pipe cleaners)
construction paper
egg carton
glue
markers or crayons
paint
paintbrush
scissors

How to Do It
1. Read a book about caterpillars and look at the illustrations or photographs. *What features do you notice on a caterpillar—legs, antennae or feelers, mouth, eyes, and so on?*
2. Cut the lid off the egg carton. Cut the carton down the middle to make two sections of six cups. Each egg carton section will be the body of a caterpillar.

3. Your child can use crayons, markers, or paints to decorate the caterpillar body.

4. Cut strips of construction paper for the caterpillar's legs. Your child can decide how many to glue to the underside of the caterpillar.

5. Cut a chenille stick in half. Help your child poke holes in the carton where the antennae should be. Thread the chenille sticks through the holes.

Beautiful Butterfly

Learn about the life cycle of a living thing by making models—now create a butterfly!

Great Books to Read Before Doing This Activity

Arabella Miller's Tiny Caterpillar by Clare Jarrett
Butterfly House by Eve Bunting
Monarch Butterfly by Gail Gibbons

What's Needed

chenille sticks (pipe cleaners)
clothespins
food coloring or paints
newspaper (to cover table surface)
paintbrushes or eyedroppers
paper towels

How to Do It

1. Cut a half sheet of paper towel for your child.

2. Mix food coloring or paints with water.

3. Spread a newspaper on your work surface.

4. To make the butterfly wings, your child can paint a design on the paper towel. The clothespin will be the body of the butterfly; your child might want to paint that, too!

5. To join the butterfly and wings, help your child pinch the middle of the paper towel and clip it with the clothespin. Your child may want to trim the edges of the paper towel so it looks more like butterfly wings.

6. Cut a 5"–6" piece of chenille stick for your child. By folding it in half and clipping it at the end of the clothespin, it can become the antennae of the butterfly.

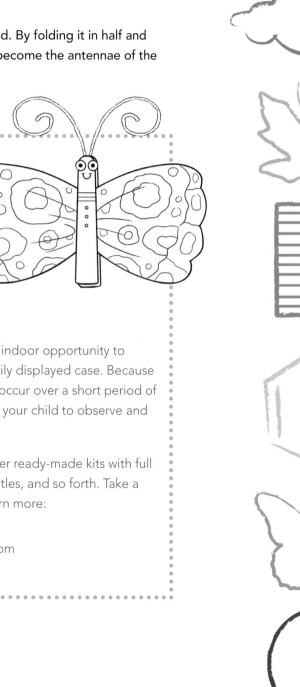

Life: It's All about the Cycle

An animal life cycle—the cycle from birth to death—is often a lengthy process that makes direct observation difficult. However, learning about the complete life cycle is an important early concept for children and their understanding of life.

A butterfly life cycle kit provides a dramatic indoor opportunity to observe a complete life cycle in a large, easily displayed case. Because of the distinct stages and the changes that occur over a short period of time, this is a great opportunity for you and your child to observe and discuss the concept of a life cycle.

Biological and nature supply companies offer ready-made kits with full instructions for butterflies, earthworms, beetles, and so forth. Take a look at one of the following websites to learn more:

> http://www.insectlore.com
>
> http://www.educationalscience.com
>
> http://www.carolina.com

Birds in Our Backyard

Observe and learn about birds in your own backyard!

Great Books to Read Before Doing This Activity

About Birds by Cathryn Sill
Birds by Kevin Henkes
Take a Backyard Bird Walk by Jane Kirkland

What's Needed

binoculars
nature journal from My Own Nature Journal, page 91

How to Do It

1. Over a period of several weeks, observe the bird activity in your backyard. This can be done from a window or by going outside and standing quietly near your house on a porch or patio.

2. Talk about the birds you see:

   ▸ *What color is the bird? What kind of markings do you observe?*

   ▸ *Compared to other birds you have seen, is it smaller or larger?*

   ▸ *How many different kinds of birds can you identify?*

   ▸ *Which species are the most numerous? Which do you see just once in a while?*

   ▸ *Which birds come in pairs?*

   ▸ *When do you see more birds—in the morning, afternoon, or evening?*

3. Use a simple backyard bird guide or check the Internet to identify some of the birds you see. The National Audubon Society website is useful for learning more about the birds that live in your area. You can find it at http://www.audubon.org.

4. Encourage your child to draw and color pictures of the birds you see, and ask her to dictate comments and observations that you can write in her nature journal.

5. If your child would like to learn more about birds, consider joining the Great Backyard Bird Count. See the website at http://www.birdsource.org/gbbc/kids for more information.

How to Explore the World of Science

Bibliography

Index

How to Explore the World of Science

To understand the world around us, scientists gather, organize, and analyze information. You and your child can use the same skills, called *process skills*, to understand the world of science. You and your child will find yourselves working like scientists as you do the following:

▶ Ask scientific questions, such as, *What is that? How did it happen? What if...? How many...?*

▶ Communicate your discoveries to other people through talking, drawing, or simple charts;

▶ Design and make models of creatures or objects that you are investigating;

▶ Estimate and predict how much, how big, how small, how heavy, how fast, how many, or what will happen next;

▶ Experiment with different ways to solve a problem or reach a goal;

▶ Find patterns and relationships as you notice repeating sequences and how one thing can influence another;

▶ Measure and compare sizes, temperatures, and weights, and use numbers to quantify your measurements. Young children enjoy measuring using spoons, straws, shoes, and other everyday items, which are nonstandard units of measure, as well as using feet and inches, which are standard units of measure;

▶ Observe and gather information by using all your senses—touch, smell, taste, sight, and hearing—to explore and learn about things and events;

- Sort and classify by noticing similarities and differences, and group objects based on similarities (also called shared attributes or characteristics);
- Use simple science tools, such as magnifiers, eyedroppers, balances, and binoculars, to explore and investigate.

We use the processes and skills of science every day because they help us explore the world in a meaningful way. This list of skills and processes is a handy reference tool to use as you explore this book. Consider reviewing the list every once in a while after you have done some activities with your child. You will be surprised at how many skills and concepts you use every single day!

The Science Content Areas

Use these scientific skills to learn about the four content areas of science:

- Design Technology
- Earth and Space Science
- Life Science
- Physical Science

Design Technology

Design technology is about the many ways people, and now computers, design tools, machines, and other inventions to solve problems big and small. Here are some ways you and your child can explore design technology:

- Ask questions: *How can we build it? What is it made of? How can we change it?*
- Take apart a broken telephone or clock, and name the different pieces. Experiment with using the pieces in new ways.
- Change a building project to make it more stable or taller.
- Talk about what life was like before telephones, television, or cars.

Earth and Space Science

As young children experience soil, sand, rocks, puddles, streams, ponds, rainbows, weather, shadows, and the moon and stars, they begin to notice characteristics, patterns, and changes that are part of earth and space. Here are some ways you and your child can explore earth and space science:

▸ Look at a thermometer to decide whether or not to wear a jacket.

▸ Sort a collection of clothing according to the season, or a collection of rocks by size or color.

▸ Look for "cloud pictures" in the sky, and name different types of clouds.

▸ Investigate various ways shadows change as the sun changes its position.

▸ Explore the properties of water: solid, liquid, and gas (also called *water vapor*).

▸ Notice and talk about the sun, moon, and stars.

Life Science

Living things are a source of endless fascination for young children. Observing and talking about a variety of living things helps children learn about basic life needs (water, food), ways of moving, life cycles, habitats, growth patterns, and the interdependence of living things. Here are some ways you and your child can explore life science:

▸ Measure each other and record your heights.

▸ Plant seeds, watch them grow, and provide sunlight, water, and plant food.

▸ Use a magnifying glass to study worms, insects, or flowers.

▸ Collect and sort different types of leaves.

▸ Match and sort pictures of animals based on what they look like, where they live, or how they move.

Physical Science

As children explore the world around them, they learn about the properties of nonliving objects and materials—what they are made of, their sizes, shapes, colors, textures, weights, and temperatures. They also learn about motion, sound, and light.

Here are some ways you and your child can explore the physical sciences:

▸ Gather a collection of objects made of materials, such as stone, metal, and plastic. Examine them, talk about them, and sort them into groups based on shape, color, or texture.

▸ With your collection of objects, experiment to see which ones float and which sink.

▸ Make musical instruments out of materials such as cardboard tubes, tin plates, cans, and tapping sticks.

▸ Ask questions and compare features: *How are these materials different? How are they the same?*

Everyday Science

It's easy to incorporate science exploration into your everyday routine:

▸ Let your child investigate all kind of objects from nature, such as seedlings, shells, leaves, or rocks.

▸ Make sure there are plenty of materials for your child to use, for example: paper, markers, playdough, modeling clay, pipe cleaners, paints, (both for painting and to experiment with mixing colors), and recycled materials for inventing and building.

- Make and display charts and lists:
  - Chart the weather over the period of a week.
  - Make a chart showing how tall each member of the family is, and record changes in height over time.
  - Create a list of items that can float in water, and a list of items that sink in water.
- Help your child make drawings, models, and books about your investigations.
- Have simple science equipment available, for example:
  - magnifying glass
  - balance
  - measuring tools, such as rulers, measuring cups and spoons, and a scale
- Explore your environment together:
  - Walk around your yard or neighborhood and listen for sounds.
  - Visit your local children's museum and science or environmental center.
  - Notice the changes in one particular tree as the seasons pass.
  - Study an insect to discover what it looks like, where it lives, and what it eats.

Bibliography

This bibliography contains children's books recommended for the science themes addressed in this book. These books are just a start! Our online database is updated frequently as new books are published. Please search www.mothergooseprograms.org to find the newest titles.

Building and Construction

Burningham, J. *Mr. Gumpy's Outing*
Mr. Gumpy tries to teach his passengers the correct way to ride in a boat.

Hoberman, M. A. *A House Is a House for Me*
Lists in rhyme the dwellings of various animals and things.

Hutchins, P. *Changes, Changes*
Pat Hutchins shows, but does not tell, how blocks become whatever a child at play imagines.

Lindbergh, R. *Nobody Owns the Sky*
Bessie Coleman dreamed of becoming a pilot, and she stuck with her dream until she made it come true.

Lowell, S. *The Three Little Javelinas*
This clever and humorous tale is sure to delight children of all ages, especially those familiar with the Southwest. Dressed in cowboy duds and prepared for life in the rugged desert, these characters are more than any coyote bargained for.

Rockwell, A. *Boats*
All about boats: freighters, steamers, ocean liners, rowboats, barges, and toy boats.

Simon, S. *Let's Try It Out with Towers and Bridges*
What keeps trees from falling over? How do skyscrapers stand so tall? What makes a bridge strong? Let's try it out!

Tryon, L. *Albert's Alphabet*
Clever Albert uses all the supplies in his workshop to build an alphabet for the school playground.

Seeds and Plants

Doyle, M. *Jody's Beans*
Jody and her grandfather plant bean seeds together. He visits occasionally, but it is up to Jody to tend the beans.

Gibbons, G. *From Seed to Plant*
This is a simple introduction to how plants reproduce, discussing pollination, seed dispersal, and growth from seed to plant. A simple project—how to grow a bean plant—is included.

Jordan, H. *How a Seed Grows*
The author uses observations of bean seeds planted in eggshells to demonstrate the growth of seeds into plants.

Krauss, R. *The Carrot Seed*
A little boy plants a carrot seed. His mother, father, and big brother agree that it will not come up, but the little boy knows better.

Perkins, L. *Home Lovely*
Tiffany transplants and cares for some seedlings. With help from a friendly postman, she makes a real garden.

Richards, J. *A Fruit Is a Suitcase for Seeds*
Richards's carefully worded information provides an excellent introduction to seeds, their purpose, and growth, which should be easy for young children to grasp.

Stevens, J. *Tops and Bottoms*
Hare turns his bad luck around by striking a clever deal with the rich and lazy bear down the road.

Shadows

Asch, F. *Moonbear's Shadow*
A story of a bear and his shadow and how they work things out.

Bulla, C. R. *What Makes a Shadow?*
This book tells us how shadows are made and then encourages readers to look for shadows in a variety of places.

Hoban, T. *Shadows and Reflections*
Photographs without text feature shadows and reflections of objects, animals, and people.

Tompert, A. *Nothing Sticks Like a Shadow*
To win a bet with Woodchuck, Rabbit tries to get rid of his shadow.

Trees

Brenner, B. *One Small Place in a Tree*
A glimpse of nature in action is offered by zeroing in on "one small place" teeming with living things.

Ehlert, L. *Red Leaf, Yellow Leaf*
Introduction to the life of a tree.

Gibbons, G. *Tell Me, Tree: All About Trees for Kids*
Discusses parts of the tree and their functions, types of fruits and seeds, kinds of bark, and uses for trees.

Lauber, P. *Be a Friend to Trees*
A lot of information is conveyed in a simple text with clear line-and-watercolor illustrations as the author shows that we cannot live without trees.

Pfeffer, W. *A Log's Life*
This introduction to the life cycle of a tree presents the complex cast of characters that reside in or on the living tree as well as on the decomposing log: all the way from woodpeckers, squirrels, and porcupines to carpenter ants, millipedes, slugs, and fungi.

Weather

Branley, F. *Down Comes the Rain*
The ups and downpours of the water cycle.

Crews, N. *One Hot Summer Day*
Relates a child's activities in the heat of a summer day punctuated by a thunderstorm.

DeWitt, L. *What Will the Weather Be?*
Will it be warm or cold? Should we wear shorts or pants? shoes or boots?
Find out why the weather is so difficult to predict.

Dorros, A. *Feel the Wind*
All about wind: what causes it and how it affects our environment. This book
includes instructions for making a weathervane.

Gibbons, G. *Weather Words and What They Mean*
Temperature, air pressure, moisture, and wind are defined and illustrated in
Gail Gibbons's explanations of weather terms we sometimes misunderstand.
One page of curious weather facts concludes the book.

Hesse, K. *Come On, Rain*
A young girl waits for the rain to bring respite from summer heat.

Hest, A. *In the Rain with Baby Duck*
Mother Duck is upset because Baby Duck hates the rain, but Grampa Duck
reminds Mother that once she had to have an umbrella and little boots, too.

Shulevitz, U. *Snow*
As snowflakes slowly come down, one by one, people in the city ignore them,
and only a boy and his dog think that the snowfall will amount to anything.

Insects and Animals

Aliki. *I'm Growing!*
With her trademark simple words and delightful pictures Aliki explains how and why we grow. The discussion includes bones, muscles, and teeth, plus internal organs.

Bishop, N. *Spiders*
Simple, engaging text conveys basic information about spiders as well as cool and quirky facts.

Gibbons, G. *Monarch Butterfly*
Describes the life cycle, body parts, and behavior of the monarch butterfly. Includes instructions on how to raise a monarch.

Hickman, P. *A New Frog*
The life of a frog from conception to adulthood as seen by a little girl on her visits to the edge of a pond.

Jarrett, C. *Arabella Miller's Tiny Caterpillar*
When Arabella Miller finds a tiny caterpillar, she brings him home and feeds him lots and lots of leaves.

Rockwell, A. *Growing Like Me*
Explains how plants and animals of the meadow, woods, and pond grow and evolve, for example: caterpillars changing into butterflies, eggs hatching into robins, and acorns becoming oaks.

Sklansky, A. *Where Do Chicks Come From?*
Explains how eggs grow and develop, eventually becoming newly hatched chicks.

Index

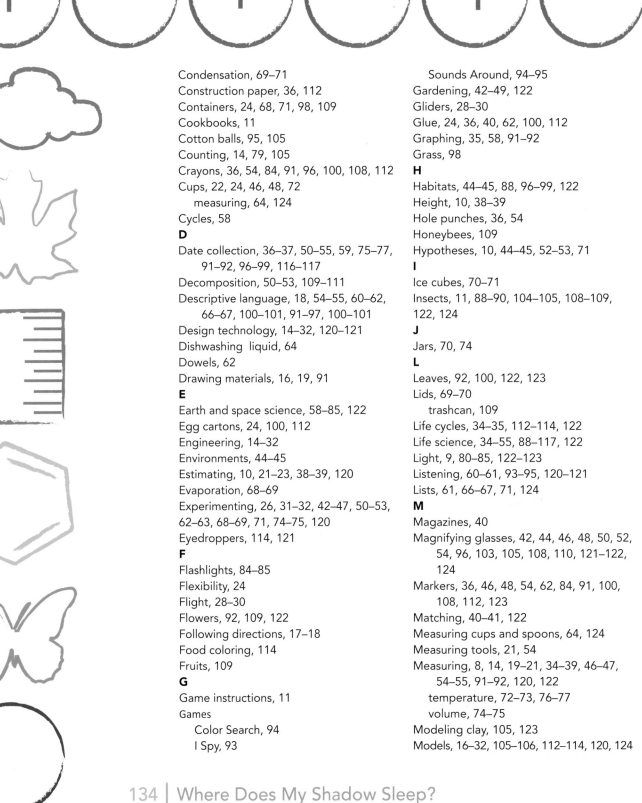

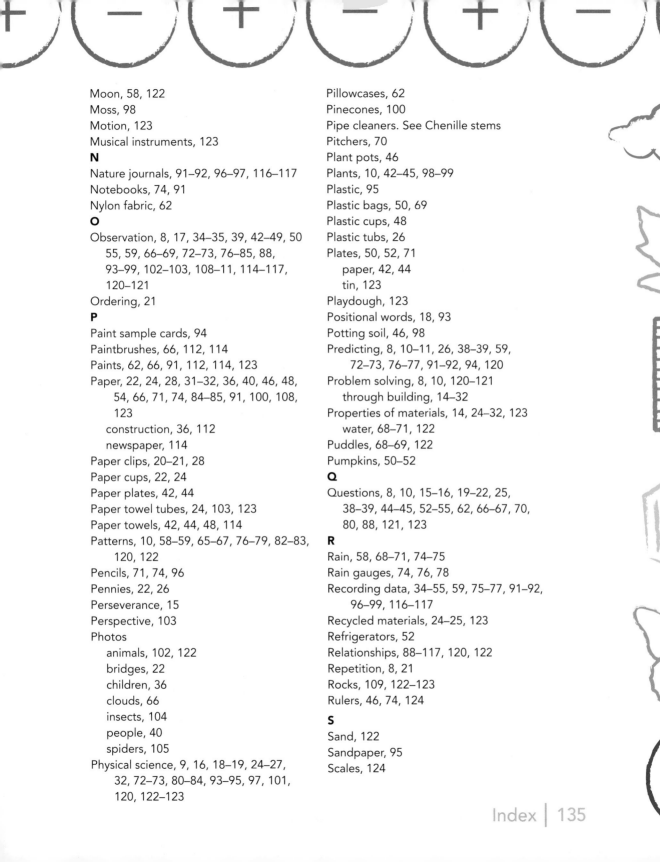

NOV – – 2012 G